I0155349

Wild Grape Jelly Sky, White Stars

poems by

Nancy H. Johanson

Finishing Line Press
Georgetown, Kentucky

Wild Grape Jelly Sky, White Stars

ACKNOWLEDGMENTS

My thanks to the following publications in which these poems have appeared:

Express Cincinnati: "The Doorway of Pear Jam"
Little Pocket Poetry: "Calling," "The Doorway of Pear Jam," "Caterpillar Zen,"
"Winter"
Best of 2014 Ohio Poetry Day: "Night Mass, Lake Erie,"
Best of 2015 Ohio Poetry Day: "Before Your Train Departs," "Lurching Forward,"
"Meanings"

Publisher: Leah Maines

Editor: Christen Kincaid

Cover Art: Nancy H. Johanson

Author Photo: Theodore L. Johanson

Cover Design: Elizabeth Maines

Printed in the USA on acid-free paper.
Order online: www.finishinglinepress.com
also available on amazon.com

Author inquiries and mail orders:
Finishing Line Press
P. O. Box 1626
Georgetown, Kentucky 40324
U. S. A.

Table of Contents

To my husband, Ted,
dear companion beyond words,
and to our wonderful children and grandchildren

Calling

Wild grape jelly sky
white stars.
I stand below on sand
blowing across Sahara's dark
desert dunes of night.
No *Little Prince*[1]
with golden hair
I do love
the rose and sheep.
I am silver haired
a woman waiting
attending the world's tiny tent.
Inside glowing
in infinite space
The One of Many Names
asks me to lift the flap
for those who journey
from anywhere
to here and back.
It is my task in life
and I like lifting
the bit of ancient hide
just high enough
so they can see
Light shining.

A View of Mary Cassatt's *Young Girl in the Garden*

From the open guidebook
I'm taken first by her young face
the calm she conveys
a countenance beyond age.
In her hands, even French lace
lights up the room.

> A critic writes:
> "The painting comes alive,
> by virtue of the calculated tension
> between the delicate draftsmanship
> with which face and hands are rendered
> in the center and the simplification
> of her pale blue dress."[2]

But what about the red flowers?
What about the sunny slope of grass
that somehow shines our old world inside out?
What about the blue cotton dress,
how draped across her ample lap
it allows the gathering of such light?

The Doorway of Pear Jam

In the palm of my cupped hand
I held a golden pear
and at its slender neck began
to peel in ribboned layers

down its curving body
till firm flesh underneath
revealed its simple beauty
white, moist, sweet.

I took another in my hand,
a green and golden pear.
This time the task that I began
lightened with each layer

as if I knew its body
the secrets underneath
and dripping with its beauty
the whole world now is sweet.

Migrations

For twenty miles
we're parked with hundreds of drivers
on the packed interstate.
I sigh, ask
"How long are we going to be stuck *here*?"

> A monarch crosses
> in front of my quiet car.
> Alive, not smashed
> it flits into a sunny field
> of summer grass.

We move at last
pass the burned out cab
its trailer seared in half,
the guard rail a melted mess.
I whisper, "*Where* is the driver?"

Spring Hermitage

Why are You summoning me now
in this hermitage of illness
where You visit me secretly,
when at last, at peace, I hear Your voice?

When all else is wrung from me,
my special plans torn open,
plowed under, buried in brown furrows
that turn startling green,

when I can bear being with You alone.
I struggle with Your presence,
preferring daughter and son
mother and father to You.

I do not leave them willingly
to walk beside You now.
Always I choose impermanence
samsara, familiar faces I love.

All are canceled for moments with You,
in this holy enclosure called Surrender.
"Canceled!" I scrawl across my mind.
You are patient. You know in the trembling freshness

of this wild April wind I will taste You.
I will let myself be found and held.
Beneath all activity, I will briefly
offer You my opened hand.

Lurching Forward

I grab a stranger's seat and steady myself.
The air is heavy with forty bodies.
Folks squirm and sigh as they try to sleep.
Neck crimped, back stiff, I start off again.

The door between cars clatters open and closed.
I enter the dome car 6:00 a.m. empty.
Soon a crooked orange ribbon
cracks the eastern rim of sky.

Blue-black clouds split
reveal a jagged dagger of light.
I think of Sean, soft spoken and slender,
the young man from Chicago's south side

whom I sat beside before searching
for a place to write. The tables were packed—
people playing poker, drinking beer
and calling home—so I came back.

Sean looked up from his book, smiling.
"I'm glad you told me why you left," he said.
"I didn't want you to think it was personal."
"Thanks. But don't work on your laptop. Relax."

He points to the biggest rainbow
I've ever seen.
We lean and look out other windows
in search of new translations of color and light.

Caterpillar Zen

It didn't matter that the world rumbled by
heavy footfalls, doorbells
keys clicking in the lock.
Even the stench of compost
black spinach and onions rotting
by the door in a pot
did not deter him.

He lay quiet and awake
aware of sun,
the coolness of shaded brick,
stretched on the lip
of a green garden shoe,
an elegant jewel
elevated just above
the mud crusted treads.

White diamonds
on his fuzzy black stripe
flanked by bands of cobalt blue,
he did not move.
He watched the world and me,
his mind clear
of a need to be busy,
of any dream of juicy leaves.

Crazy Ass Sky

Thunderstorms rear up
ranging wildly
rush across our
agile skies.

Lightning crouches
snaps white fingers
neon pounces
in my eyes!

Tank-like rumblings
wake me, shaking.
I wonder faintly
is it War?

I fumble cringe
lights slice darkness
like men at market
chop meat or more.

Windows rattle
bird nests teeter.
The dogs cry
at our bedroom door.

I let them in
grab prayer beads
and jump down under
the covers once more.

Landfall

The man on the radio described a hurricane
reaching landfall at 70 miles an hour.

It was in Mississippi or Louisiana
and the storm was named Isadore.

I thought, what a beautiful name for wind,
Isadore.

What does landfall mean, I wondered
driving through fog toward home.

Is it landfall when a butterfly touches down
on the petal of a flower?

When lovers' feet touch the ground just slightly
is that landfall too?

Is it landfall when armies reach a foreign shore
weapons strapped on tight as wristwatches that leave a mark?

And is it landfall now when my fingers touch these keys
and words float out like dust?

Attention Writers

After drenched hills
I pass
Penfield
Pennsylvania
and imagine
a field of pens
or a sylvan grove
of growing pencils.
I laugh
and learn that Paperville
near Erie
is real.

Temple

Walking by November trees
in the cemetery
we stop astonished
so late in the season
a rose bush
before us
in full bloom.

Circling
without prayer wheels
without bowing
I smell each bloom
then pick one
a pink bud
a Buddha.

Meanings

After dinner on Epiphany
I pack up ornaments and leave
our naked tree huddled
in the living room forest
of cactus, ficus and hibiscus.

Overnight a red flower appears
dangling in front of the pine
where the Christmas star
shone all last week.

Generous old hibiscus
your wild arms reach like Kali
to wrap your one branch
with a bright red bloom
around our dying tree.

Next night your spent blossom
dark purple, furled tight
around tired golden stamens
drops and is caught and cradled

in a pine needle nest.
A new red bud unfurls
where the Christmas angel
had been! Who are you,
I marvel, grabbing a dictionary.

"Hibiscus is used in worship
of Devi, female aspect of God.
It is the flower of Kali."
To me it means miracle,
bearer of red, rebirth, mystery—

Farewell

Wrapped in white cloth
King Abdullah
is lit by the sun.

At the entrance to the mosque
his body is raised.
The pallbearers pause.

Each man's head is covered
perhaps comforted
by a red checked headdress.

One man lifts his hand
wipes his eyes.
They carry the body inside.

The call to prayer sounds.
Reverent men and women
kneel and bow.

Before the men lift him
before they take recess with his body
one woman leaves her place

in the front row.
She comes close.
The folds of her white headdress

blend with his shroud.
Her hand hesitates in mid air—
She touches him.

Waiting Night After Night

Down the long dark
past reeds on the dock
I go with no light
but my longing.

Black swirling water
below me familiar
Milky Way clear
I gaze like a child.

Then suddenly *there*
strange lime green flares
spurt into the sky
in bright arcs.

Shimmering, pulsing
this necklace rippling
light so exquisite
my balance is lost.

Afraid of falling
I reach for a piling
grab hold, grip tight
till the light disappears.

Winter Night

Leaning close to the woodstove
I peel off wet jeans
drape long johns over an iron poker
white sails on a Chinese junk.

I yank the clothes away
before they burst into flame.
In the kitchen
fry bread smells buttery hot

and cozies the cold cabin.
"The stars" he says
stamping snowy boots
"are big tonight."

Under a Roof as Thin as Light

Coastal mists whisper secrets
in far off places like Marin.
Blue ethereal Mackinac dazzles
island jewel of Michigan.
And, in Cornwall's sea coast outpost—
Merlin's fair immortal haunt—
they say that faerie magic charms us,
dissolving worldly boundaries.

But I'm just driving in Kentucky
north on route four seventy-one.
A summer Sunday—steamy ordinary
I'm sipping coffee the radio on
same old landscape coming home.
Then I notice, past the windshield,
every hill is strangely beaming
trees are turquoise, the air is cream.

Squinting and staring
I hold the wheel steady,
steer past hills before the bridge.
Is it humidity
some strange serendipity
this shining view before me opening?
Crossing the Ohio River
I see Cincinnati as borders thin.

"Mt. Adams, it's luminous!
Eden Park shimmers,"
I shout, aware of an ancient force.
Of course, I know I'm in Ohio
but all around me so amazing
is the presence of all this light.
Call it Avalon, call it Heaven,
I'm grateful to be welcomed in.

O Solstice Gate

By our only sea, the inland sea
where waves mix playfully with dream,
my love and I kick off our sandals,
wading. Water laps our ankles.

Splashing near us, making ripples
children hurl their shore rocks flying.
Seagulls skim the waves while crying,
"The longest day is now, and dying."

But one girl with a sidearm swing
sends her flat stones lightly tripping,
past the sunset they keep skipping.
I was called by inner priest or priestess

far from roads to see great Phoebus, and
I found this beach to behold both zenith
and sun descending hills of evening
lavender, slate-blue and soothing

as Old Sol's path to us is fading.
And black as bark, small fishing boats
hug the horizon's edge afloat.
Above them, fiery orange Apollo

prepares to be received by Water,
plummets softly, gently enters
the mystery waiting at the center.
In silence we behold and stand,

our toes imprinting cool damp sand.
Eyes lowered as this day ends
yet holding hands, we look again
and bending, gather up our stones.
Having seen, we journey home.

An Errand in Lessening Light

If it weren't for her, you mutter,
you wouldn't make this crazy trip
You carve the mountain miles slowly,
at first savor the icy tresses flowing
from cracks in stony faces.
A lonely field yields frozen music—
lines of snowy furrows meet
ragged cornstalk notes.

Suddenly a sign appears:
Coal Keeps The Lights On.
Strewn cinders, stripped tires
mark the hard scrabble highway
pocked with potholes wide as a car.
Sheets of clean snow shear off
speeding semis and slap
sooty roadside drifts.

You tell yourself to drive on.

And you need hope at midnight when
you near the roaring Brooklyn traffic,
and horribly high Verrazano Bridge.
You cuss your way across.
"They don't call it *The Narrows* for nothing,"
someone said. Semis rush past,
then squeeze in front of you.

Entering Brooklyn, you can't read
directions in the dark.
You pull off the highway lost.
You find a corner store gas station
to ask for help. But the guy
behind the counter motions
he doesn't speak English.

Suddenly, four kids surround you.
"Sixteenth street? Yeah, I know it.
Get her a pencil, Joey.
Don't get back on the highway.
Just turn there, see? Keep going.
You don't mind a lot of lights, do ya?"

Before Your Train Departs

Leave your belongings
at the old station.
Walk the twisted brick path
past the vacant lot
where Galesburg's water tower rises
in the middle of white clover.
Follow the signs
past half a mile of tiny yards
to the white cottage.
Look all the way through
the three room birthplace
of "Charlie" or Carl
who quit school after eighth grade
to deliver milk
lay brick
heave coal
thresh wheat
shine shoes
travel as a hobo
work for a paper [3]
so he could write Chicago Poems.

"toil, struggle, blood and dreams, among lovers . . .
workers, loafers, fighters, players, gamblers . . .
 the lovedand the unloved, the brutal and the
compassionate —one big family hugging close to the ball
of Earth for its life and being."[4]

Then come out back.
See the red granite rock
beneath the sycamore?
It marks his ashes.
Stand a moment
before you leave
to catch your train.

Lotus Is Their Name

Where pine ridges leap
and their precipice
meets Lake Hope,
I grab Sky, our old kayak,
hidden among the lilies
behind the plank dock.

I step in, tip and cast off.
We glide quickly
from the world to quiet.
Behind me, fishermen
become small as children.
I pull hard to cross this bay.
Piercing the sharp breeze
I thread the needle.

More and more water lilies
—are they lotus flowers?—
grow on this side.
With each lift of my paddle,
lines of silver drops slide
down the blade onto me.
I follow fuschia lilies
through prussian blue waves
to the deeper water.

How can a lily pad float out here,
I ask, tugging a thick stem,
like pulling up a great anchor.
I wonder how far down
till it reaches rock bottom?
Taut and strong, it doesn't give.
I finally let go.

Splashing into fierce wind
my shoulder burns, cries
"Slow down. It's a long slog
back to the dock."
But I don't stop—
because just ahead
in the far narrows
floating cities of hot pink
welcome me.

Here all waves subside.
I pause, pray, and enter
this quiet water
its zone of color.
Someone told me
the lake ends near here.
In a tiny creek,
not far,
it simply disappears—

Night Mass, Lake Erie

If you look far, across the dark water
the tiny white lights of towns now glimmer.
The black bridge becomes red flickering flashes
votive candles upon this night's altar.

Chilled purple clouds chase our torn sky
lake waves, steel blue, pound seawall sides.
Black branches thrash, wild grace in this wind
as red disappears into night.

Come in from the cold, you who wander.
Take your place by the hearth, good sister, brother.
Fill your glass with red wine and sit, quiet poet,
words fly like sparks from the fire.

Notes

1. *The Little Prince,* a novella by Antoine de Saint-Exupery, was published in 1943 by Reyna! & Hitchcock (U.S.) and Gallimard (France). It is interesting to note that *The Little Prince* was voted the best book of the 20th century in France and translated into over 250 languages and dialects. This beloved classic has sales of over 140 million copies worldwide.

2. Quote from a guidebook from the Musee d'Orsay in Paris.

3. Quote from Wikipedia, Carl Sandburg entry, Life section.

4. Quote by Carl Sandburg in *The Family of Man,* 1953, published by Jerry Mason

My Thanks

Many thanks to Jeff Hillard, poet and mentor, for his generous help with preparing my manuscript for publication.

I am grateful to poet Annie Stapleton for her mentoring, and for her sensibi I ities which I treasure.

My thanks to Ann Townsend, poet and teacher, who years ago at the Antioch Writers Workshop first encouraged me by saying, "It's refreshing to meet a poet who doesn't call herself one."

I'm thankful for poet friends for their inspiration and critiques, and grateful to many friends near and far for their camaraderie and support.

My thanks to Leah Maines, publisher of Finishing Line Press, to Christen Kincaid, my editor at Finishing Line, and to Elizabeth Maines for her design help with my chapbook cover.

An artist, poet and energy healer, **Nancy Johanson** is also the mother of five grown children.

Her childhood home was nestled in an apple orchard just outside the city. She recalls climbing up into a beloved, old tree with a fat, lower branch where she sat to watch the sky. Nature still is a source of deep wonder and beauty—a spiritual treasure to her.

In her early twenties, Nancy co-founded The Cincinnati Waldorf Children's Center and furthered her interest in the work of Rudolf Steiner. She began studying art while her children were small and sold her paintings, cards and drawings in England, New Hampshire and locally at The Cincinnati Public library and the Cincinnati Art Museum gift shops, local cafes and restaurants.

At midlife, Nancy followed an inner calling to return to school for a masters in pastoral counseling. She worked as a therapist and then discovered energy healing work which opened new pathways of healing for her clients.

Nancy earned certificates from The Barbara Brennan School of Spiritual Healing, The Peacemaker School of Spiritual Healing, and in Reiki, Light Body, and Flow Alignment and Connection. Nancy maintains a healing practice today.

Her book, *Light Showings: Moments In Divine Presence*, was published in 2013. It offers visionary experiences from the turn of the new millennium when she sat in prayer and meditation; and was invited across the veil into a deeper dimension of reality some would call heaven.

Nancy is currently rewriting a novel for young adults, called *Day Dreamer*. Visit Nancy's website at: nancyhjohansonpoems.com

www.ingramcontent.com/pod-product-compliance
Lightning Source LLC
LaVergne TN
LVHW041329080426
835513LV00008B/654